Did you know ...

Welsh Sports

interesting

strange

amazing

incredible

excellent

cool

This Pont book was first published in Welsh in 2013 by
Gomer Press, Llandysul, Ceredigion, SA44 4JL
under the title *A Wyddoch Chi am Chwaraeon Cymru?*

ISBN 978 1 84851 981 7

A CIP record for this title is available from the British Library.

This book is published with the financial support of the
Welsh Books Council.

Printed and bound in Wales at
Gomer Press, Llandysul, Ceredigion

The publishers would like to thank the following for giving permission to reproduce images in this publication:

Front cover: Alamy (epa european pressphoto agency b.v.), Photolibrary Wales (Andrew Orchard), Shutterstock (Neil Wigmore)

Alamy: 6 (Associated Sports Photography), 7 (Allstar Picture Library; Associated Sports Photography), 8 (epa european pressphoto agency b.v.; Jeff Morgan 08), 12 (David Edsam), 14 (Gallo Images), 15 (Jeremy Inglis), 17 (Allstar Picture Library), 18 (david pearson; ALLSTAR Picture Library), 19 (Eleanor Parsons; Leo Mason sports photos), 20 (CTK), 22 (epa european pressphoto agency b.v.), 23 (Jeremy Inglis), 24 (Allstar Picture Library; Jeremy Inglis), 25 (ALLSTAR Picture Library), 26 (epa european pressphoto agency b.v.), 27 (epa european pressphoto agency b.v.; Peter Llewellyn), 28 (Galen Rowell/Mountain Light), 29 (Archive Pics), 30 (UK City Images), 32 (David Curtis; Sport In Pictures; Everett Collection Historical).

Alun Morris Jones: t. 26

PhotolibraryWales.com: 7 (Andrew Orchard), 11 (David Williams), 12 (Mike Dean; Andrew Orchard), 13 (Andrew Orchard), 14 (Huw Jones), 15 (Jeff Morgan), 19 (Glyn Evans; Andrew Orchard), 21 (Andrew Orchard; Ceri Breeze), 22 (David Williams; Glyn Evans), 23 (David Williams), 26 (Andrew Orchard), 27 (Glyn Evans), 29 (Steve Peake).

Shutterstock: 6 (Neil Wigmore), 9, 10 (photogolfer), 13 (Rosli Othman), 14, 15, 16, 17, 20, 22, 23, 24, 25, 27, 28, 29, 30, 31 (NEIL ROY JOHNSON),

Logo: 6 (Y Dreigiau; Y Gleision; Y Gweilch; Y Scarlets).

Did you know . . .
Welsh Sports

Alun Wyn Bevan
Translated and adapted by Cathryn Gwynn
Cartoons by Eric Heyman

Pont

SHARP

Contents

Rugby

Did you know …

- ★ The first rugby ball was made of a pig's bladder!
- ★ The Welsh Rugby Union was formed in Neath in March 1881.
- ★ Seven-a-side rugby was added as one of the sports for the Rio de Janeiro Olympic Games in 2016.

- ★ There used to be letters on the back of players' shirts!
- ★ But numbers were placed on Wales shirts from 1922.
- ★ By now, the players' surnames are also on the shirts.

★ Wales has four professional regional rugby teams:

- **The Dragons –** Newport and Gwent
- **The Blues –** Cardiff, Pontypridd, the Valleys and south Powys
- **The Ospreys –** Neath, Swansea, Aberavon and Bridgend
- **The Scarlets –** Llanelli, the west and mid-Wales

Fact!

A club game was postponed in 1966 because nobody had brought a ball!!

★ The name of our national rugby ground in Cardiff has changed three times:

- The Arms Park
- The National Stadium
- The Millennium Stadium

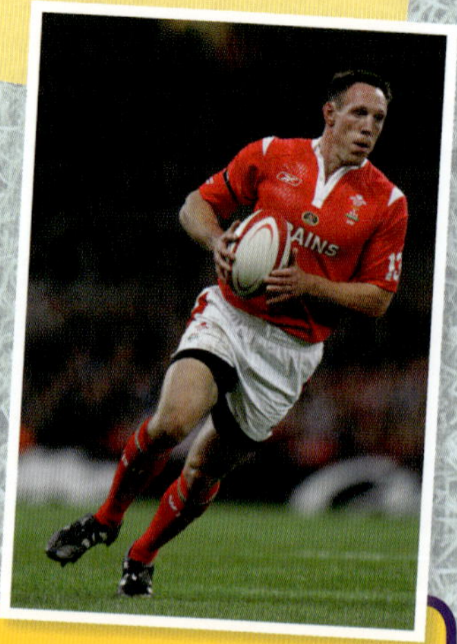

Vocabulary

bladder: a sack within the body which holds waste fluid

regional: something which belongs to an area of a country

postpone: to put off until a later date

Q+A

QUESTION: Who scored the first try at the Millennium Stadium?

ANSWER: Mark Taylor – in a game between Wales and South Africa in 1999.

Did you know ...

George North

Colin Charvis

Gareth Edwards

Welsh World Records

- ★ **George North** is the youngest to score a try in a World Cup game (19 years old).
- ★ **Colin Charvis** is the forward who has scored the greatest number of tries (22).
- ★ **Gareth Edwards** played 53 consecutive games for his country, and he was the first Welshman to win 50 caps (1978).
- ★ **Paul Thorburn** kicked the longest ever penalty kick (64.2 metres) in a game between Wales and Scotland in 1986.

Shane Williams

- ★ Experts and fans believe that Shane is the best winger ever to represent Wales.
- ★ Shane scored 60 international tries (58 for Wales and two for the Lions) – the greatest number ever for a European player.

Fact!

Shane Williams' father placed a £50 bet on his son being the scorer of the greatest number of tries for Wales one day. He won £25,000 when Shane scored try number 41!

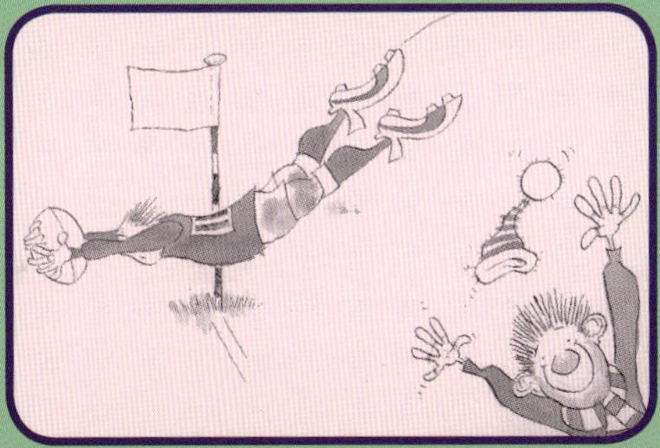

Record	Name	Age	Year?
The youngest to win a cap for Wales	Tom Prydie	18 years and 25 days	2010
The youngest to score a try in his first game for Wales	George North	18 years and 214 days	2011
Wales' youngest captain	Gareth Edwards	20 years and 7 months	1968
Wales' youngest World Cup captain	Sam Warburton	22 years and 341 days	2011
Wales' youngest forward to win 50 caps	Alun Wyn Jones	25 years, 10 months and 18 days	2011

Vocabulary

consecutive: one thing following another
international: relating to more than one country

Did you know ...

The World Cup

- Wales reached the semi-final of the World Cup in 2011 for the first time since 1987.
- Wales' best score in a World Cup game was 81-7 against Namibia in 2011.

Unlucky Players

- Arthur Buchanan – 1876 – the Llanelli Rugby Club captain died when he slipped on the edge of a wall and accidentally shot himself while hunting ducks.
- Henry Jarman – 1910 – the international forward from Wales died after jumping in front of a coal tram to save the lives of a group of children.
- Jean-Pierre Salut – 1969 – he tripped on the stairs on the way to the field in the Stade Colombes in 1969 and broke his ankle.
- Gaston Vareilles – 1910 – on his way to Paris to win his first cap for France, he stepped off the train to go and buy a *baguette*. The train departed without him – and he never played for the Tricolor again!

Fact!

A few minutes before winning his first cap in 1975, the centre Ray Gravell was in tears after receiving a telegram from Twdls, the cat, wishing him well!

Vocabulary

semi-final: the last round but one
accidentally: happening without meaning to
departed: left

Q+A

QUESTION: How many series have the Lions won in New Zealand?

ANSWER: Only one – in 1971, under the leadership of the Welsh trainer, Carwyn James.

Golf
Did you know …

* There are 176 golf courses in Wales.
* The Welsh Golfing Union is the second oldest union in the world.
* The oldest golf club in Wales was formed in Tenby in 1888.
* Golf was added as one of the sports for the Rio de Janeiro Olympic Games in 2016!

Fact!

Golf has been played on the moon, and there are still two balls up there!

* Each golf hole has to be exactly 4.25 inches (11 centimetres) in diameter.
* Golf balls travel further on warm days!

Vocabulary

diameter: the distance across a circle, going through the middle

Q+A

QUESTION: How many dents are there on an official golf-ball?

ANSWER: 336

Did you know ...

Becky Brewerton

- She is the only Welsh woman to win a place in the European team in the Solheim Cup competition, which is the female version of the Ryder Cup.

Ian Woosnam

- Ian Woosnam and David Llewellyn won the World Cup for Wales in 1987.
- Woosnam has represented Wales more than 15 times in the World Cup.

- He was the first person from Europe to win more than $1 million dollars (about £640,000) in one season!
- He was number one in the world in 1991.
- He was introduced as 'Ian Woosnam from Wales, England' when he won the Masters Championship in the USA in 1991. He received an apology.
- He played in eight consecutive Ryder Cups between 1983 and 1997.
- As the Europe captain, he led his team to victory in the 2006 Ryder Cup.

Q+A

QUESTION: Why did a meeting of the Tenby Town Council finish early in 1875?

ANSWER: The Mayor had arranged to play a round of golf in the afternoon!

Vocabulary

version: something which is similar, but slightly different

represent: to do something or speak on behalf of someone else

Did you know ...

The Ryder Cup

- Only six holes-in-one have ever been hit in the Ryder Cup.

- Children under five years old are not allowed to go to the competition.
- Six golfers from Wales have competed in the Ryder Cup so far – Bert Hodson, Dave Thomas, Dai Rees, Brian Huggett, Ian Woosnam and Phillip Price.

The Celtic Manor

- The Ryder Cup was held in Wales for the first time in October, 2010.
- The Celtic Manor course in Newport was the venue.
- The course cost £16,000,000 (£16 million) to create.
- It took five years to be developed.
- 1.1 million tons of earth were shifted.
- As the course was created, several archaeological finds were made, including Roman pottery and graves.
- Wales' First Minister, Carwyn Jones, opened the tournament officially.

Q+A

QUESTION: Why did the Ryder Cup go on into the the fourth day for the first time ever in 2010?

ANSWER: Because of the poor weather!

Vocabulary

venue: a place where events are held

archaeological: to do with the study of the remains of man from the time before history was recorded

finds: discoveries

tournament: a series of competition rounds until a champion wins

Football
Did you know ...

- ★ Wales is the third oldest international football team in the world.
- ★ The Racecourse stadium in Wrexham is the oldest international stadium in the world which continues to hold international games.
- ★ Cardiff is the only team from Wales to win the England Cup.

Q+A

QUESTION: How many Welshmen have scored in the final rounds of the European Cups?

ANSWER: Four – Mike England, Mark Hughes, John Hartson and Simon Davies.

The Premier League

- ★ Swansea's club, the Swans, is the only team from Wales to reach the England Premier League.
- ★ The club received £90,000,000 (£90 million) following their promotion in 2011.

Fantastic Footballers!

Ryan Giggs

- ★ **Ryan Giggs** was the first Welshman to score a goal in the Millennium Stadium.
- ★ He has appeared 963 times for Manchester United, and he is now their assistant manager.
- ★ He scored 168 goals for the team.

Gary Speed

- ★ **Gary Speed** was the first player ever to appear 500 times in the Premier League.
- ★ **Mark Hughes** was the first to win the Professional Footballers Association (PFA) Player of the Year award twice – in 1989 and 1991.
- ★ Ian Rush, Mark Hughes, Ryan Giggs and Gareth Bale are the only other players from Wales to have won this award.

Mark Hughes

Vocabulary

promotion: to rise to a higher level
award: prize

Did you know ...

Record	Name	Age	Year?
Wales' youngest scorer	Gareth Bale	17 years and 35 days	2006
The youngest to play for Wales	Gareth Bale	16 years and 315 days	2006
The oldest to play in a game for Wales	Billy Meredith	45 years and 229 days	1920
Wales' youngest captain	Aaron Ramsey	20 years and 90 days	2011

Aaron Ramsey

Gareth Bale

- If Gareth Bale were transferred to another team, he could be worth about £95,000,000 (£95 million).

Fact!

In 2011, Robbie Savage wore 72 football shirts all at the same time – this is a world record!

Q+A

QUESTION: What is the distance between two football goal posts?

ANSWER: 5.64 metres

Cricket

Did you know ...

- The first official cricket game in Wales was played in 1793 on common land at Cwrt Henry in Carmarthenshire.

Glamorgan County Cricket Club

- The Glamorgan Cricket Club was formed in 1888.
- This is the only cricket club which has represented Wales in the County Championships since 1921.
- The club won the Championship in 1948, 1969 and 1997.
- The SWALEC Stadium in Sophia Gardens, Cardiff is the main home of the Glamorgan cricket team.

SSE SWALEC Stadium

Matthew Maynard

Q+A

QUESTION: Which players have scored the greatest number of runs in the history of the Glamorgan County Cricket Club?

ANSWER:

1.	Alan Jones	34,056
2.	Emrys Davies	26,102
3.	Matthew Maynard	22,764
4.	Gilbert Parkhouse	22,619

Fact!

In 1993, Mathew Maynard succeeded in scoring 100 runs before lunchtime against Australia at the Gnoll in Neath.

Vocabulary

common: a piece of land which everybody has the right to use

Q+A

QUESTION: Where is the highest cricket pitch in Wales?

ANSWER: Bethesda, Gwynedd. On a clear day, you can see the peaks of Tryfan, Carnedd Dafydd and Carnedd Llywelyn from up there!

Did you know ...

- **Robert Croft** is the first Welshman to score 10,000 runs and take 1,000 wickets in first class cricket.

Fact!

The SSE SWALEC Stadium in Cardiff was home to the opening match of the Ashes series in 2015.

Past games

- In a game on the St.Helen's ground in Swansea in 1969, Garry Sobers hit six sixes in an over. He was the first to achieve this.
- Derryth Lynne Thomas from Llanelli represented the England women's cricket team between 1966 and 1982.

Fact!

A large tree grows in the middle of the cricket ground at Narberth. When the ball hits the trunk or a branch, four runs are awarded to the batsman.

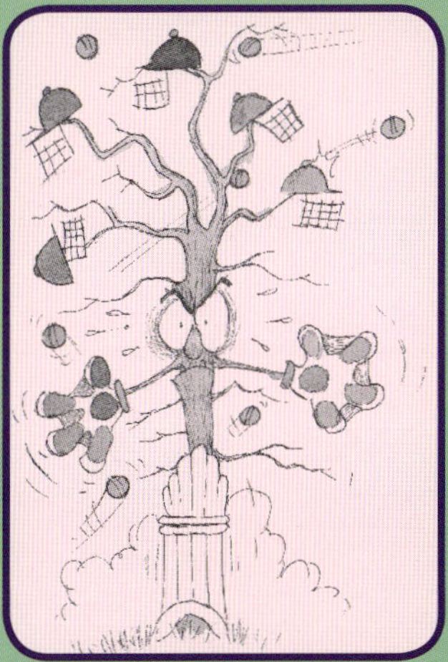

Vocabulary

over: a bowler bowls a ball six times to the batsman in an over

Tennis

Did you know ...

- A Welshman, Major Walter Clopton Wingfield, invented lawn tennis in 1873 in order to entertain his guests at parties!
- Tennis can be played on grass, on a clay court or on a hard court.
- The main competitions in the tennis world are
  - Wimbledon – grass court
  - The French Open – clay court
  - The Australian Open – clay court
  - The US Open – hard court

Grass court

Clay court

Hard court

Fact!

Michael Davies is the only Welshman to reach the Wimbledon finals, and that was in the men's doubles.

Q+A

QUESTION: Why did Venus Williams from the USA, lose a point in the Australian Open Championship in 1999?

ANSWER: Because a string of beads had come loose in her hair and had scattered across the court.

Vocabulary

lawn: a piece of smooth mown grass

scatter: to spill everywhere

Did you know ...

- In 1972, tennis balls changed from being white to an optical yellow so that television viewers could see them more clearly on the screen.
- Each ball is filled with air so that it bounces better.
- 300,000,000 (300 million) tennis balls are produced every year.

- Wimbledon tennis balls are recycled to make nests for harvest mice.

Fact!

After losing in the boys' singles comeptition in Wimbledon in 2011, Evan Hoyt from Llanelli played tennis with Rafael Nadal to help him practise his game for the final round of the championship!

Q+A

QUESTION: Who was the first British person in 76 years to win the US Open Championship in 2012?

ANSWER: Andy Murray

Vocabulary

produced: made
final: last

Athletics

Did you know ...

The Olympic and Paralympic Games London 2012

- All the bronze, silver and gold medals for the Olympic Games in London 2012 were produced at Llantrisant near Cardiff!
- These are the biggest and heaviest Olympic medals ever!
- Each medal is 85 mm in diameter.
- It took ten hours to create each medal.
- The Welsh won:
  - Seven medals in the London Olympic Games (three gold medals and four silver).
  - 14 medals in the London Paralympic Games (three gold medals, three silver and eight bronze).

Rhys Williams

- Two Welshmen competed in the 400 metres hurdles race at the Olympic Games in London 2012:
  - Dai Greene from Llanelli (world champion, 2011)
  - Rhys Williams from Bridgend (European champion, 2012)

Dai Greene

- He won a gold medal in the World Championships in 2011, in Daegu, South Korea.
- He won a gold medal in the European Championships in 2010 in the the 400 metres hurdles race in Barcelona.
- He won a gold medal in the Commonwealth Games in 2010 in Delhi, India. His time was 48.52 seconds.
- Dai Greene was the captain of the British team in the London Olympics in 2012.

Vocabulary

hurdle: a light gate which is placed on the track in a race so that runners have to run and jump over it

Did you know ...

Aled Siôn Davies

★ In the London Olympic and Paralympic Games, Aled, from Bridgend, won:
- a gold medal for throwing the discus (46.14 metres).
- a bronze medal for throwing the shot-put.

Nathan Stephens

★ He won a gold medal in the javelin competition at the Paralympic Athletics World Championships in New Zealand in 2011.

★ He broke the world record throwing the javelin 41.37 metres in 2011.

★ Nathan and Aled Siôn train side by side.

Baroness Tanni Grey-Thompson

★ This paralympic athlete has won:
- 11 gold medals
- three silver medals
- one bronze medal

★ She won the London Marathon six times between 1992 and 2002.

Helen Jenkins

★ She was number one in the World Championships in 2008 and 2011.

Kirsty Wade

★ This middle-distance runner from Llandrindod was the first female to win the BBC Wales Sports Personality of the Year award in 1986

★ She has won three gold medals in Commonwealth Games.

Did you know ...

Lynn Davies

- He was the first Welshman to win an individual Olympic gold medal, for the long jump in Tokyo in 1964.
- He was the first athlete to hold on to Olympic, European and Commonwealth titles at the same time.
- He jumped further than eight metres 21 times. In 2009, only two athletes from Britain succeeded in jumping further than eight metres.

Fact!

Thousands of people gathered together in Nant-y-Moel to congratulate Lynn on his success, and he thanked them through his bedroom window!

How does Lynn Davies' distance in the long jump compare with other winners?

Enw	Olympic Games	Distance
Lynn Davies (Britain)	Tokyo (1964)	8.07 metres
Bob Beamon (USA)	Mexico City (1968)	8.90 metres
Carl Lewis (USA)	South Korea (1988)	8.72 metres

Vocabulary

individual: single, not part of a group or team
congratulate: to tell someone warmly how well you think they've done

Did you know ...

Colin Jackson

- Colin held the world record for the 110 metres hurdles race for 13 years (between 1993 and 2006!)
- 12.91 seconds was his record time.
- He also holds the world record in the 60 metres indoors hurdles race (his time was 7.30 seconds in 1994).
- He won a silver medal in the Seoul Olympic Games in 1988.
- He did not succeed in winning an Olympic gold medal.
- He was world champion twice – Stuttgart 1993 and Seville 1999.
- He was champion in the Commonwealth Games twice – Auckland 1990 and Victoria 1994.

Q+A

QUESTION: On which television series did Colin Jackson dance in 2005?

ANSWER: Strictly Come Dancing – and he came second in the final!

- Many competitors lost their way in thick fog and ended up running over 20 miles in a half marathon (13 mile) race at Newton-Aycliffe, County Durham.

- **Josef Barthel** from Luxembourg – 1952 – Helsinki Olympic Games. When he won the 1500 metres race, nobody had prepared the music for the Luxembourg national anthem for the winners' ceremony.
- **Jesse Owens** – 1936 – Berlin Olympic Games. He won four gold medals, but when he went to a New York hotel for a dinner held in his honour, he had to use the servants' entrance because he was a coloured person.
- **Fred Lorz** – 1904 – St.Louis Olympic Games. He was on the verge of receiving the gold medal for winning the marathon when it became known that he had travelled 12 miles of the race in a car!

Vocabulary

honour: to show respect and congratulate
verge: edge

Swimming
Did you know ...

★ After athletics, swimming is Wales' most successful sport in the Olympic and Paralympic Games.

Cardiff International Pool

Q+A

QUESTION: How many 50 metres Olympic length swimming pools are there in Wales?

ANSWER: Only two:

- The Cardiff International Pool
- The Wales International Pool in Swansea.

Fact!

Women's swimming costumes looked quite different many years ago!

Ellie Simmonds

★ The paralympic champion, Ellie Simmonds, practises in the Swansea pool.

★ Ellie was only 13 years old when she won two gold medals for Britain in the Beijing Paralympic Games in 2008.

★ Ellie is the youngest person ever to receive an honour from the Queen.

★ She won two gold medals, one silver and one bronze in the London Paralympic Games, 2012.

Vocabulary

honour: award with praise

Did you know ...

Olympic medals

- **David Roberts** swam in seven competitions in the Sydney Paralympic Games (2000) and won seven medals.
- After his success in the Beijing Paralympic Games in 2008, the swimmer has:
  - 11 gold medals
  - Four silver medals
  - One bronze medal

Fact!

David Roberts holds the record in the 50 metres, 100 metres, 200 metres and 400 metres free stroke swimming competitions.

- The swimmer **David Davies** from Barry (Dai Splash to his friends), won a bronze medal at the Athens Olympic Games (2004) and a silver medal in Beijing (2008).

- **Irene Steer** from Cardiff was the first Welshwoman to win a gold medal in the Olympic Games, in Stockholm in 1912.
- Her team won the free style over 100 metres relay in the best time ever recorded.

- **Paulo Radmilovic** from Cardiff was the first Welshman to win a gold medal at an Olympic Games.
- He won four Olympic gold medals between 1908 and 1924 for water polo.

Cycling
Did you know ...

- ★ There are about 1,000,000,000 (1 billion) bicycles in the world – twice the number of cars.
- ★ You can park up to 20 bikes in the space needed to park just one vehicle.
- ★ The first bikes were designed without pedals!

Nicole Cooke

- ★ Nicole Cooke is the first from Wales to win an individual Olympic gold medal since 1972.
- ★ She won a gold medal in the women's road race in the Beijing Olympic Games in 2008.
- ★ She was the second woman from Wales to win a medal following Irene Steer's success in 1912.

Geraint Thomas

- ★ Geraint Thomas won a gold medal with the British team in a track cycling event in the Beijing Olympics when he was 22 years old, setting a world record of 3 minutes 53.314 seconds.
- ★ He was the youngest competitor in the Tour de France race in 2007.
- ★ He wore the White Jumper, which represents the best young cyclist (under 25) of the competition, for four days in the Tour de France, 2011.
- ★ Geraint won his second Olympic gold medal in London, 2012. In a track race, Geraint and his team set a world record time of 3 minutes 51.659 seconds over a distance of 400 metres.

Vocabulary

represents: stands for

Hockey

Did you know ...

Q+A

QUESTION: What are the measurements of a hockey field?

ANSWER: 92 metres long and between 50 and 55 metres across

- Only the goal keeper is allowed to use their feet to kick the ball.
- The sport is played in 70 countries around the world, and on all continents.
- Wales won the bronze medal in the European Championships 2009.

Fact!

Sports historians believe that hockey was played for many years before the days of Christ.

Sarah Thomas

- Sarah, from Merthyr Tydfil, was a member of the British women's hockey team which won the bronze medal in the London Olympic Games, 2012. She was the only Welsh woman in the team.
- Sarah scored the last goal in the British victory (3-1 against New Zealand).

Vocabulary

continent: one of the seven enormous areas of land on the face of the earth

victory: a win

Great Achievements

Did you know ...

Q+A

QUESTION: How much time do the people of the Arctic have to go outside to use the toilet before things begin to freeze?

ANSWER: 30 seconds!

Lowri Morgan

- ★ She competed in a 222 kilometres race across the Amazonian jungle.
- ★ She lost all her toenails and suffered from trench foot.
- ★ She competed in the 633 Ultra Race in the Arctic in temperatures of –92°C.
- ★ Only six people have ever completed this challenge.

Jade Jones

- ★ Jade is the first person from Britain to win an Olympic gold medal in Taekwondo (London, 2012).

- ★ She is the second Welshwoman to win an individual gold medal.
- ★ Her nickname is 'Headhunter'.
- ★ She won the BBC Wales Sports Personality of the Year Award in 2012.

Non Evans

- ★ Non is the individual who has represented Wales in the greatest number of sports – rugby, judo, wrestling, weight lifting and power weight lifting.
- ★ She was honoured by the Queen for her contribution to the sports.

Water Sports

Did you know ...

Rowing

- ★ There are two kinds of rowing:
  - one is where the rower holds an oar in both hands
  - one is where the rower uses both hands to pull one oar through the water
- ★ Rowing is one of the few sports which uses all the main muscles of the body.
- ★ **Tom James**, from Wrexham, was a member of the British coxless four team which won a gold medal at the London Olympics, 2012.
- ★ **Chris Bartley** and his crew won a silver medal at the London Olympics 2012 in the rowing competition for a lightweight men's four.

Tom James

Chris Bartley

Elin Haf Davies

- ★ She was the first Welshwoman to row across the Atlantic Ocean.
- ★ She was also one of the first team of women to row 3,200 miles across the Indian Ocean in 2009, setting a world record.

Fact!

Rowing is one of the few sports where the competitors cross the finishing line backwards!

Sailing

- ★ A sailing boat is the name for a boat which uses a sail for moving through the water rather than oars or engines.
- ★ Sailors use the power of the wind to change the direction and speed of the boat.
- ★ **Hannah Mills**, from Dinas Powys, won a silver medal in the the sailing race for women pairs at the London Olympic Games, 2012.

Climbing
Did you know ...

Q+A

QUESTION: After which climber from Powys was the highest mountain in the world named?

ANSWER: Sir George Everest

- **Caradog Jones** was the first Welshman to reach the summit of Everest in 1995.

- **Tom Whittacker** was the first disabled person to reach the summit of Everest in 1998.
- The Welshman lost a part of his leg in a road accident in 1979.

Tom Whittaker

- **Tori James** was the first Welshwoman and the youngest British woman to conquer Everest.
- She was a member of the women's team which had competed in a race to the North Pole in 2005, pulling sleighs over frozen seas.
- **Richard Parks** is the first person ever to climb the highest mountain on each of the seven continents, as well as the two poles, in around six and a half months.

Vocabulary

summit: the highest point

poles: north and south points at both ends of the Earth's axis

Did you know ...

- **Edgar Evans** from Rhosili was one of the members of Captain Scott's voyage to the Antarctic in 1912.
- He was one of the five who succeeded in reaching the South Pole, but the entire crew perished.

- **Eric Jones** was the first British person to climb the north face of the Eiger in 1969.
- At 63 year old, he jumped off the highest waterfall in the world, the Angel Falls in Venezuela. He is the oldest person to do this.
- In 1991, as one of a four man team, he flew two balloons over Everest. This was recorded in the Guinness Book of World Records.

Fact!

Eric Jones has also done stunt work for James Bond films!

Vocabulary

perish: to die
record: to make a formal note of something

Horse Racing

Did you know ...

Chester Race Course

Racing courses

- There are three racing courses in Wales:
  - Bangor on Dee in the North-East
  - Chepstow on the banks of the Wye river
  - Ffos Las in Carmarthenshire
- Chepstow is Wales' largest race course.
- Ffos Las opened in June 2009 on the site of old open coal mine works.
- Chester, in England, just over the border with Wales, is:
  - the oldest race course in Britain – horses have raced there since the 16th century
  - the shortest course – it is only a mile and a furlong in length

Ffos Las Racing Course

Wales Grand National

- The Wales Grand National was held first in 1895 on the course at Ely, Cardiff.
- It is held between Christmas and the New Year.
- In 1980, Linda Sheedy was the first woman to compete in the race.

Fact!

Jack Anthony won the British Grand National three times with Glenside (1911), Ally Sloper (1915) and Troytown (1920).

Vocabulary

furlong: an old way of measuring distance (8 furlongs = 1 mile)

Did you know ...

These are the Welshmen who have won the Grand National since the Second World War.

Name	Where from?	How many times did he win the Grand National?	The name of the horse, and in which year?
John Cook	Gwent	1	*Specify* (1971)
Neil Doughty	Kenfig Hill	1	*Hello Dandy* (1984)
Hywel Davies	Cardigan	1	*Last Suspect* (1985)
Carl Llewellyn	Pembrokeshire	2	*Party Politics* (1992) and *Earth Summit* (1998)

Famous Horses

- *Norton's Coin* – in 1990, Norton's Coin, a horse from Nantgaredig, surprised everyone when he won the Cheltenham Gold Cup on odds of 100/1.

Fact!

During the last fifty years, 36 horses have been killed after being injured in the Grand National race.

Boxing
Did you know ...

How many matches has every boxer won or lost?

		Win	Lose	Extra Information
Jim Driscoll	(1880-1925)	54	3	He fought 15 rounds when he was 39 years old, with his left hand thumb completely dislocated. 100,000 people attended the funeral of the world's unofficial champion.
Jimmy Wilde	(1892-1969)	137	4	He was a world champion for longer than anyone else. His nickname was 'The Mighty Atom.'
Howard Winstone	(1939-2000)	61	6	He lost the tips of three fingers on his right hand in his teens after an accident in a toy factory. He was world champion for six months.
Colin Jones	(1959-)	26	3	He was the youngest British boxer to compete in the Olympic Games, before Amir Khan in 2004. He competed in the Montreal Olympic Games in 1976.
Joe Calzaghe	(1972-)	46	0	He was world champion for more than 11 years.
Nathan Cleverly	(1987-)	24	0	He was the world Light-heavyweight champion from 2010–2013

★ **Fred Evans won a silver medal in the Welter weight competition in the London Olympics, 2012.**

Q+A

QUESTION: Which boxer from Wales was known by the nickname 'The Tonypandy Terror'?

ANSWER: Tommy Farr – one of the most well known boxers in Wales and England at one time!

Fact!

It's more than likely that **Freddie Welsh** (1886-1927) is the only vegetarian to win the World Championship in the world of boxing.

Vocabulary

dislocate: to come loose, to undo
unofficial: informal, not having authority